Rock Climbing

GET OUTDOORS

Neil Champion

WAYLAND

First published in 2008 by Wayland

Copyright © Wayland 2008

Wayland
338 Euston Road
London NW1 3BH

Wayland Australia
Level 17/207 Kent Street
Sydney NSW 2000

Senior editor: Jennifer Schofield
Designer: Rachel Hamdi and Holly Fulbrook
Photographer: John Cleare – www.mountaincamera.com
Photoshoot co-ordinator: Hannah Wilson
Proofreader: Susie Brooks

Acknowledgements:
The author and publisher would like to thank the following climbers for
participating in our photoshoot: Nick Bentley, Charlotte Garden, Becky Hall,
Rosh Karia and Peter Whittaker. A special thank you to Phil Robins at The
Edge Climbing Wall in Sheffield, England www.sheffieldclimbing.com and
DMM Internatonal, Wales for supplying equipment to be photographed.

All photography by John Cleare except
27 Ian Smith/Mountain Camera; 28 left Chris Craggs/Mountain Camera;
29 top Graham Parkes/ Mountain.Camera

British Library Cataloguing in Publication Data
 Champion, Neil
   Rock climbing. - (Get outdoors)
   1. Rock climbing - Juvenile literature
   I. Title
   796.5'223

ISBN: 978-0-7502-5060-3

Printed in China

Wayland is a division of Hachette Children's Books,
an Hachette Livre UK company.
www.hachettelivre.co.uk

Note to parents
and teachers:
The website addresses (URLs)
included in this book were
valid at the time of going
to press. However, because
of the nature of the Internet,
it is possible that some
addresses may have changed,
or sites may have changed or
closed down since publication.
While the Author and
Publishers regret any
inconvenience this may cause
the readers, no responsibility
for any such changes can be
accepted by either the
Author or the Publisher.

Disclaimer:
In preparation of this book,
all due care has been
exercised with regarad to
the advice, activities and
techniques depicted. The
Publishers regret that they
can accept no liability for any
loss or injury sustained. When
learning a new sport, it is
important to get expert
tuition and to follow a
manufacturer's advice.

Contents

What is rock climbing?

Rock climbing is a great sport for those who want a challenge, both physical and mental. It can be done at indoor climbing walls, on cliffs and up mountains the world over. Climbing uses technical pieces of equipment, made from special materials in sports laboratories, to provide the best performance and safety possible.

A growing sport

Over the past 20 years, climbing has been one of the fastest growing sports in the world. It has gone from being an activity carried out by very few people, to something enjoyed by all – from six-year olds to 60-year olds and with a variety of physical abilities. There are very few barriers to being able to take part in this sport.

Modern climbers use specially designed equipment to help protect them should they fall.

The challenge of climbing

Climbing is a very simple sport. If you take away the clutter of equipment, it comes down to the ability to use your arms, legs, balance, strength and not least your brain, to move up something that is very steep. Climbing fulfils a need for adventure and physical challenge. It is exciting and rewarding to reach the top of a climb, and the effort you put into reaching the top can be felt when you look back down to the ground. This can also be a little scary, but that is part of the thrill and the challenge. There are no limits: climbs can be short or long, easy or hard. You can climb right to the top or maybe stop halfway up if that is what you want. The important things are the experience and the enjoyment.

This climber is ascending Napes Needle in the Lake District, England, where the sport is thought to have started.

Early Equipment

Victorian climbers used only a rope for safety. The rule was: 'The leader never falls' – the climber out front relied upon skill and judgement. Over the years, more equipment was added. Slings of rope were used to put over small rock spikes and eventually, metal 'nuts' were used to place in cracks in the rock to help protect the climbers in the event of a fall.

This photograph was taken about 50 years ago. It shows two climbers in the British mountains, using limited protection and an old-fashioned rope.

The first rock climb

The first recorded rock climb took place in 1886. An Englishman named W. P. Haskett Smith climbed a pinnacle of rock in England's Lake District called Napes Needle. People had climbed before this date, but usually for specific reasons such as herding goats in the mountains or carrying out observations on plants or rocks or weather conditions. Haskett Smith clambered up his rock spire only to reach the top. There was no other reason, and so the sport of climbing rock for its own sake was born.

How to get started

Most people have a natural instinct to climb. We clamber up things even as babies, finding out about the environment around us, and continue when we are older – at school, in the park, or close to home. The things we climb might be a wall, a tree, a climbing frame, or a piece of furniture.

The first step

To start climbing as a sport, you need to find an indoor climbing wall or a rock face, or crag, outside. Ideally, this would be quite close to where you live so that you can get there easily and, more importantly, regularly. Like any sport, to become good at climbing, you need to practise as often as you can.

These girls are climbing at an indoor wall. The one on the ground is belaying (see page 11) the lead climber.

Conquering the Matterhorn

The Matterhorn, a mountain in the Swiss Alps, was first climbed by a team led by the English climber Edward Whymper, in the nineteenth century. On the way down, tragedy struck. One of the men slipped, dragging others to their deaths. Whymper was saved because the rope snapped. After this terrible event, he wrote:

'Climb if you will, but remember that courage and strength are nought without prudence, and that a momentary negligence may destroy the happiness of a lifetime. Do nothing in haste; look well to each step; and from the beginning think what may be the end.'

Clubs and societies

It is important that you find someone who can help you start on your climbing career in safety. This might be an experienced parent or older friend. Or it might be through people at a school club or society, the Scouts, or a local climbing club. The main thing is that they understand the possible dangers involved, and that they are able to take the responsibility of helping you to learn safe climbing skills.

On this real outdoor rock, an older, more experienced climber is helping young people to have a safe and exciting day climbing.

Climbing equipment

Once you have decided that you want to take up climbing, you will need to buy some basic pieces of equipment, including shoes and a chalk bag. These will ensure not only your safety but also your comfort.

Chalk bag – this is a small bag that climbers fill with powdered chalk and hang off their waists at the back. Hands can get hot and sweaty, especially when the going gets tough, so to help avoid slipping off a hand hold, you can dip into your chalk bag while in the middle of a climb. The chalk will absorb sweat and dry your hands.

Helmet – your head is the most important part of your body and needs extra protection when you climb. Falling on your head, or being hit from above by tumbling stones, could be very dangerous. Helmets are made from special, tested materials to give you extra safety.

Harness – called a sit harness, this is made from a waist belt attached to leg loops. It is very strong and has to pass special tests to prove its design and materials are safe for use. The climbing rope is attached to the harness at the front, using a figure-of-eight knot (see page 10). It also has 'gear loops' for carrying other pieces of equipment, such as karabiners (see page 9).

Rock boots – these are tight-fitting, specially designed climbing shoes. The soles are made from high-friction rubber that sticks to very small foot holds. They are not very comfortable to wear, but they will help you to get the most out of your climbing, whether at an indoor wall or outside.

Once you have the basic kit, you can start to climb with confidence. As you become more experienced, you may wish to buy more equipment. For example, in order to climb high, you will need to be attached to a rope and you will also need karabiners and belaying devices for safety.

Belay devices – these are used to apply a braking action to the rope to hold a falling climber or lower him or her safely to the ground.

Rope – this is a very technical piece of kit. It has two main parts: very long nylon threads and a tough outer sheath. The sheath protects the threads. The rope is designed to stretch a bit so that the energy from a fall can be absorbed. Ropes come in various lengths, mostly between 50 and 60 metres. They also come in different widths or diameters, between 8 and 11 millimetres. All ropes have to pass special tests to meet the demands of the vital role they play in catching a falling climber.

Figure-of-eight descender – this is used when abseiling.

Screwgate karabiner – this is used with a belay device to safeguard a climber.

Other equipment includes karabiners, belay and abseil devices, slings, and protection gear for placing in cracks when lead climbing – nuts, hexes, and camming devices.

The safety chain

All the equipment climbers use to keep them safe, should they fall, is known as the safety chain or safety system. It includes the rope, harness, slings, karabiners, belay device and the gear used to make anchors and a belay. Like any chain, it is only as strong as its weakest link, so it is important that it is checked often for damage.

Putting on a harness

Make sure your harness is fastened securely around your waist and not on your hips.

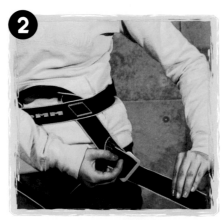

Do up the safety buckle according to the manufacturer's recommendations.

A well-fitting harness fits high on the waist and snugly tight around the waist and legs.

Attaching the rope to the harness

To attach your harness, tie a figure-of-eight knot about 1 metre down the rope. Then thread the end of the rope through the attachment points on your harness.

Now rethread the figure-of-eight knot, leaving a tail of rope about 22 centimetres.

Finish your rethreaded figure-of-eight knot with a thumb knot and pull to tighten the whole thing.

Checking Your Equipment

Make sure you check your kit for any damage. Run your hands over the rope to see if the sheath is showing any signs of wear and tear each time you use it. The inner threads are white and if you can see them poking through the sheath, it might be time to replace your rope.

Similarly, cast your eyes over your harness, helmet, slings and metal gear, such as karabiners. Manufacturers give advice on when to change your kit. This may be after a heavy fall or it might be when it is getting too old.

How strong is my kit?

All modern climbing materials are incredibly strong and light. They have to be able to hold a climber who might fall from high up. The impact involved can be huge because the force increases with the distance of the fall. You might weigh only 50 kilograms, but if you fell 10 metres, the jolt you would give to your partner holding you on the rope would feel a lot more than that. That is why some ropes are made strong enough to take the weight of a two-tonne truck.

Know-how

It is not just the strength of the equipment in the safety chain that is important. Those using the kit have to do so safely. When accidents happen, it is usually because of human error, not the equipment failing. Therefore, it is vital that you know how to put on a harness correctly, how to tie the rope safely into the harness, and how you use the belay device.

Using a belay device

1 Communication between the climber and belayer and good belay technique are essential.

2 As your climber ascends, he or she will produce slack rope, which needs to be taken in.

3 Pull down on the 'live' rope and up on the braking rope at the same time.

4 Lock the rope off by pulling down on the braking rope.

5 Place your 'live' rope hand on the braking rope, and move your other hand up to join it.

6 Place your 'live' rope hand back on the live rope and you are back to where you started.

As in any sport, you will climb better if you warm up your muscles before you start. You will also help to avoid injury to muscles, tendons and joints if you have a gentle routine to prepare your body. Do not forget, once you have finished your climbing session, make time to do some simple stretches again. This will prevent you from having sore muscles the next day. Stretching helps to repair any damage done to muscle fibres and helps them to bounce back for use the next time you want to go climbing.

Stretch your fingers and forearms by straightening each arm in turn and pulling the fingers back gently.

You can stretch your forearms by placing your hands together in a praying posture and gently pushing them down while lifting your elbows up.

Warming up

The best way to prime your muscles ready for the stresses of climbing is to do some gentle aerobic exercise. This can be in the form of jogging or cycling to the climbing wall or crag. Or it can be running on the spot or skipping when you arrive. In fact, any form of exercise that makes your heart beat faster sending blood around your body and into your muscles will do the job. Aerobic exercise will make your lungs work harder and plenty of fresh oxygen will be pumped around your body.

Progressive Climbing

After you have warmed up and done some basic stretching, do not leap straight on to the hardest parts of the rock. Make sure you start gently, using the biggest hand and foot holds you can find. This continues the process of getting your body ready for harder things to come. Aim to be climbing at your hardest by the middle of your session and then ease off towards the end. This way, you will climb harder and for longer and you will also have less tired muscles the next day.

These climbers are doing a variety of stretches for the arms and shoulders. It is important to stretch gently and to hold each pose for 15 seconds or more.

Stretching

You can do some gentle stretching before you start to climb, but the most benefit comes from stretching after you have finished. Make sure you stretch your forearms, shoulder joints, elbows, wrists and fingers properly because these are the areas of high wear and tear when you climb. It is also a good idea to stretch your back and hamstrings. Muscle fibres get damaged when you use them energetically, but stretching them helps to repair this damage and avoid too much soreness the next day.

Using indoor climbing walls

Indoor climbing walls provide one of the best ways to start rock climbing. They can be used all year round, come rain or cold weather. This is important because it means you can climb whenever you want to.

At the wall

You can find climbing walls in most towns and cities. They tend to be friendly places where you can meet other climbers with whom to practise and learn from. Many climbing walls run clubs and courses specifically aimed at young people. There will need to be an adult at the wall who will take responsibility for you while you climb. Many climbing walls run a policy of 'climbing for all', and trained staff will be able to help anyone who wants to try the sport but has a disability.

This young person is bouldering on the artificial wall of an indoor climbing centre. Bouldering is a useful way to warm up and stretch the limbs – stick to easy moves when you are doing this.

Bouldering

Climbing without any rope or harness is called bouldering. It began when people walked up to boulders in the mountains and used them to improve on their climbing skills. The idea is that you never climb very high, so if you fall off, it does not matter and you are unlikely to injure yourself. You simply get back on and try the move again. Bouldering enables climbers to try and retry hard moves and so build up their strength and endurance. Most indoor climbing walls have an area specifically used for bouldering. These climbs are not high and there is usually a large, spongy mat on the floor to cushion a fall.

Learning the ropes

At the main part of a climbing wall, ropes and harnesses are essential. These may be provided by the people who run the wall, or you may need to bring your own. The idea is to climb as high as possible, knowing that in the event of a fall you will be tied to a rope to prevent injury. The most important thing is to climb with someone who knows how to belay properly, and who you can trust. This means that you can relax as you climb higher, which helps with your climbing technique.

Climbing in the roped area of a wall will also help to develop your climbing strength and endurance. All climbing walls have routes that have been given a grade. You can choose easy, moderate or hard grades to try to climb.

Learning to Lead

Most climbers will at some stage want to have a go at leading, although it is by no means for everyone. Leading means climbing your chosen route, clipping protection as you move up. It is the most exciting part of climbing – a real mini-adventure. Do not feel forced into doing it – you have to want to have a go. This is because there is greater risk involved. It is very different to bottom roping because the rope is not above you. You can fall 2–3 metres if you come off, which can be scary.

This is called bottom roping. The belayer stands on the ground, taking the slack rope in as the climber ascends the wall.

Climbing on real rock

All the skills and techniques that you learn climbing indoors can be put to good use outside, too. You can boulder or use ropes to climb higher routes.

The differences

Climbing outside is different. For a start, you have to be weather-wise. Rain makes the rock more slippery and dangerous. A strong wind can blow you off balance. Cold temperatures can leave your fingers like blocks of ice, with little feeling left in them. Make sure you know what weather to expect, and take the right clothes along to cope with it.

There are also different types of rock. Granite is hard and can be rough and grippy. Slate is smooth, but has positive edges. This means that your fingers and feet feel secure when using the holds. Limestone is steep but has good holds. Gritstone can be quite rounded but because it is rough, it gives good friction. You will need to develop the ability to 'read the rock', both for its particular climbing qualities and for where the holds might be. Indoors, the holds are often marked in vibrant colours, but outside, there are no such clues. It is all up to you to work out!

Climbing on sea cliffs with the sound of crashing waves below you can be one of the most exhilarating experiences.

These climbers are in the mountains of Snowdonia in North Wales, one of the great places in which to practise the sport.

Height Matters

Climbing outdoors is far more varied than indoors. Not only does the rock present different challenges, but the venue is also important. You can climb on sea cliffs from Cornwall in England to Thailand and Spain. Here dramatic views out across the waves combine with local bird life to give a very adventurous and wild feel to the climbing.

You can climb on smaller crag outcrops, the most well-known being the gritstone edges in Derbyshire. Or you can choose to climb in high mountains on longer routes. The Highlands of Scotland, the Alps in Europe and the Rocky mountains in the USA are examples of fantastic places to do this, provided you do not mind long walks to get to the routes! These climbs can be several hundred metres high. They are called multipitch climbs (as opposed to the single pitch climbs found on smaller crags and cliffs). Tackling a big mountain route is about as exciting and daring as it gets.

Outdoor climbing routes can be very long and high, and while this may seem nerve-racking it is also very exciting.

Technique and movement skills

It is important that you learn good technique from the start. Good footwork, being aware of your balance and neat and precise moves are all crucial to success. Also, learning how to find resting places on a route and being able to calm your mind are important skills to master.

Climbing efficiently

The more efficiently you learn to climb, the more energy you save. This means you can climb harder routes for longer periods of time. Practise climbing the same route repeatedly, but try to do it differently each time. Then try to work out which way felt better and easier. Was this because you used your feet in better positions, or kept your body close to the wall? Come up with some answers and then put them into practice on another climb to see if they work again.

This climber is using a technique called bridging. With a foot on either side of the crack, he can get a 'hands-free' rest, remaining in balance with his weight over his feet.

Using your feet

One of the main techniques in climbing is to use your feet to maximum potential because your feet and legs form the basis of your climbing. Legs are far stronger than arms, so it is more efficient to push up using your thigh muscles than to pull up using your fingers and forearms.

This climber is using her feet well. Her weight is over her left foot, which is positioned in a small, horizontal crack.

Obviously, climbing uses both hands and feet to gain height, but you should aim to use your feet and legs as much as possible. To do this, you need to trust your feet and you need to learn to use them like precision instruments. Think of climbing as a special vertical dance, where neatness and balance are just as important as strength and courage.

Games of balance

You can work on your balance at the climbing wall. Find an easy slab to climb. Now scrunch your fingers into a fist, so that you cannot use them on the holds. The idea is to climb a little way up the wall using only your feet and leg muscles to push off, rather than using your hands to pull up. You can place your fists on the wall, but do not curl your fingers around any hold. As you move up, concentrate on your foot placements. Make small movements only, transfer your weight onto one leg, push up and place your other foot on a hold. Do not go any higher than it is safe to fall off from. Make sure the safety mat is always below you.

Using all your limbs now, you can try closing your eyes and making a few simple movements close to the ground. Have a friend stand by to tell you where the holds are. Try to focus your attention on your body. What can you find out about how you are moving from one hold to another?

This climber is using a technique called smearing. He has placed his feet with as much of the sole touching the rock and his weight is out and pushing in towards the climb.

Building strength and endurance

To build strength, climbers do circuits and practise difficult moves at the climbing wall. To be a good climber, you also need to eat healthily and drink enough water to keep hydrated.

Bouldering circuits

Circuits are a mixture of moving up, down and traversing around the wall or a small section of rock outdoors. The idea is to stay on the wall or rock for as long as possible, going around in one direction. This will help to develop not only your climbing technique, but also your endurance. You will be able to climb for longer without becoming too tired. While doing circuits, look for natural hands-off rests. These will probably be in a corner where you can bridge out your feet in a wide stance and lean into the wall with your body. You should then be able to take your hands off to have a shake-out, to get blood and energy back into your arm and hand muscles.

This climber is bouldering outside using a crash mat. He is working on short, difficult moves to improve his technique and strength.

Bouldering indoors doing circuits is a good way to warm up and to improve your endurance.

Food for sport

If you want to get the most out of your climbing, pay attention to what you eat and drink. Carbohydrates, found in wholegrain bread, pasta, rice and potatoes, provide slow-burning energy. Foods high in protein, such as meat, chicken, beans, fish and cheese, enable your muscles to repair themselves after heavy use. Aim to eat a wide variety of food that includes vegetables and fruit. You will need to drink plenty of liquid when you are climbing hard, especially when the weather is hot. Physical performance drops dramatically if you become dehydrated. Isotonic drinks provide energy and salts quickly, but water or diluted juice are good, too.

Short, hard moves

To help increase your strength, you can find a sequence of moves on the wall that are possible but hard for you. Try this only when you are warmed up. Climb the sequence as slowly and with as much control as you can. If you fall off, take a good rest to regain your full strength, then have another go. Try to extend the number of hard moves that you can make at any one time before you fall off. Once these hard moves no longer feel so tough, make a new sequence that feels hard. In this way, you will be developing the muscles needed to climb harder and harder moves.

The person on the ground is 'spotting' the other climber – protecting her should she fall off the wall, though not aiming to catch her.

Using holds well

Climbing harder and longer routes is all about developing your technique and strength to cope with the demands put upon you. It is also about learning to conserve energy and control some of the fear that might be rising in your mind at the time.

Dealing with steep rock

Whether climbing indoors or outdoors, you will need to learn how to use hand and foot holds to their best advantage. Climbers have developed lots of specific words to describe the holds and the type of move you can make using them.

Jamming – using a thin crack to find a hand jam. This technique involves expanding your hand inside the crack to wedge your hand in.

Crimps – using this technique on a small hand hold is called crimping. The thumb is placed on top of the index and middle fingers to help protect and strengthen them.

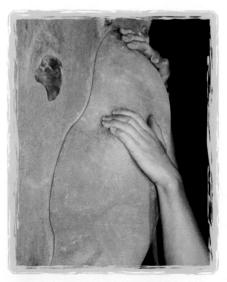

Slopers – using two open hands on a large, sloping hold. This demands strong fingers and forearms.

Jugs – curling the fingers around a large hold, often referred to as a jug or 'thank God' hold!

Egyptian – this climber has his left hip into the rock and his back knee is bent. This allows him to keep his weight over his feet on steep rock.

Heel hook – this climber uses a heel hook with her left leg. It enables her to stay balanced and use a strong, straight left arm to move upwards.

Laybacking – this uses the opposing forces of the climber's arms pulling out, and his legs and feet pushing into the rock to get up an awkward, vertical crack.

Dealing with a Fall

All climbers fall at some stage. This may be in the relatively safe zone of bouldering, or bottom roping or climbing while seconding. You should never fall very far in any of these situations, so try to stay as relaxed as you can. A tense body is more likely to get injured. Also, try to control the fall by using your hands and feet to protect yourself when landing. If bouldering, then make sure you bend your legs and roll over to avoid spraining an ankle. It is useful to take a few deliberate falls at an indoor climbing wall, just to get used to the feel of it. If you do this, make sure you do so safely.

Taking a leader fall can be more serious. However, provided you have protected the climb well, you should not sustain any injury. The rope will stretch and absorb the energy and cushion you, even if you fall some distance. It is important that you avoid hitting anything. Push yourself away from the rock face if you can.

As this boulderer falls onto his crash mat, he is away from the wall and looking at where he will land.

Abseiling

Abseiling is the skill of sliding down a rope while remaining in control of your speed and safety. This is done using an abseil device that creates friction to act as a brake.

When to abseil

There are lots of situations when you might need to abseil. For example, if you are climbing on a cliff, you may need to abseil to the bottom if there is no path down, to be able to start your climb back up your chosen route. If you are on a multipitch route and it starts to rain, forcing you to retreat, you may need to abseil down.

Abseiling can be a lot of fun. However, it needs to be done correctly and safely. Make sure, if you have a go, that you double-check anchors, your harness and abseil device before you go over the edge.

This abseiler is ready for take-off. She is using a safety rope (the blue one) to help her gain confidence in abseiling.

Ready for take-off

To abseil safely, the rope should be attached to a strong and dependable anchor such as a tree, spike of rock or bolts. The free end is then thrown down the cliff face – make sure it reaches the ground. You will need to have your harness on and be wearing your helmet.

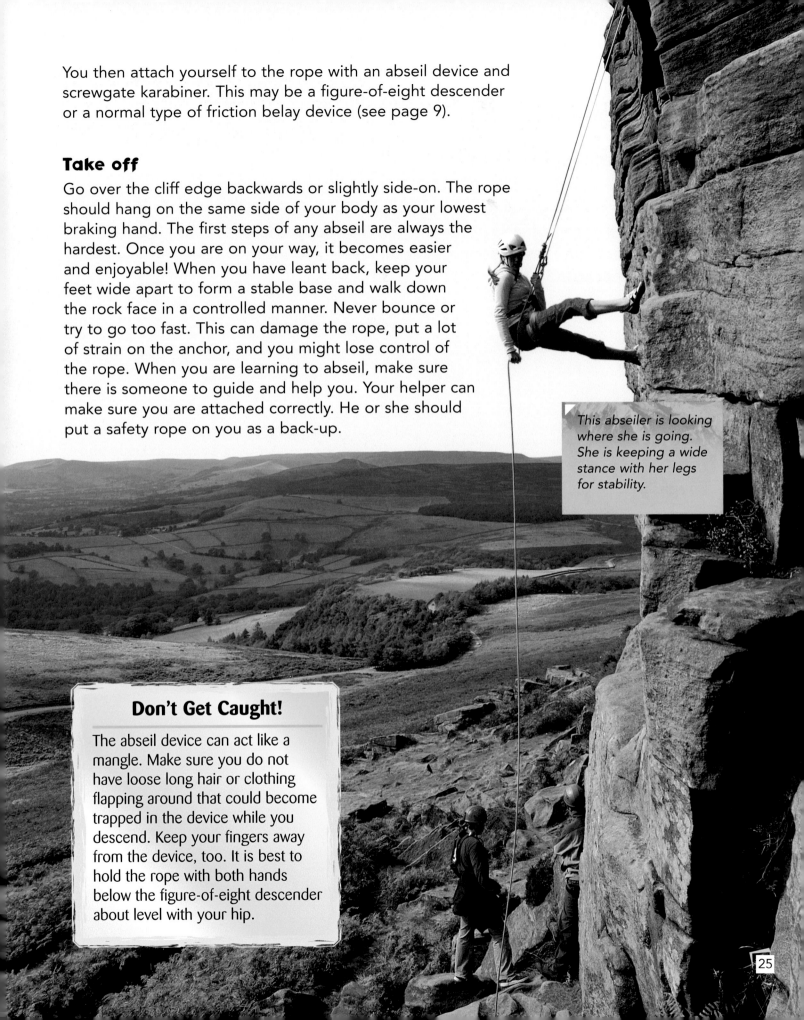

You then attach yourself to the rope with an abseil device and screwgate karabiner. This may be a figure-of-eight descender or a normal type of friction belay device (see page 9).

Take off

Go over the cliff edge backwards or slightly side-on. The rope should hang on the same side of your body as your lowest braking hand. The first steps of any abseil are always the hardest. Once you are on your way, it becomes easier and enjoyable! When you have leant back, keep your feet wide apart to form a stable base and walk down the rock face in a controlled manner. Never bounce or try to go too fast. This can damage the rope, put a lot of strain on the anchor, and you might lose control of the rope. When you are learning to abseil, make sure there is someone to guide and help you. Your helper can make sure you are attached correctly. He or she should put a safety rope on you as a back-up.

This abseiler is looking where she is going. She is keeping a wide stance with her legs for stability.

Don't Get Caught!

The abseil device can act like a mangle. Make sure you do not have loose long hair or clothing flapping around that could become trapped in the device while you descend. Keep your fingers away from the device, too. It is best to hold the rope with both hands below the figure-of-eight descender about level with your hip.

Taking part in competitions

Taking part in climbing competitions has grown along with the rise in popularity of indoor climbing walls. Today, there are lots of opportunities to compete at all levels and in different age groups.

Getting involved

Competitions can involve bouldering, lead climbing and speed climbing. There is something to suit everyone. Most competitions have categories for junior and senior climbers as well as male and female entrants. You can ask at your local climbing wall to find out if there are any competitions in the region. Often, climbing walls have their own league championships for bouldering or lead climbing. You can also contact local climbing clubs or your national mountaineering council, such as the British Mountaineering Council (BMC), for information. Competitions are a great way in which to meet other like-minded climbers and to test yourself against them.

Taking part in an indoor bouldering competition can be strenuous but very rewarding.

BRYCS

The British Regional Youth Climbing Series (BRYCS) is run by the BMC. It is open to all 7–15 year-old climbers around Britain. Each age category has male and female competitions, first as regional rounds and then at a national final, where the winners from the regional rounds climb against each other.

This woman is taking part in an indoor lead climbing competition. The routes are made increasingly difficult for the competitors as the tournament progresses.

Rock around the world

Rock climbing is enjoyed all around the world by people from all walks of life. For example, you can climb straight off the beaches in parts of Thailand, or tackle huge mountain rock faces in Nepal or Pakistan. You can travel into the desert of Jordan or Morocco to climb sun-baked crags, or dodge the showers on a Scottish mountain. There is a world of adventure at all levels, from relatively easy and accessible climbs to the very hard and remote.

Climbing in Britain

British rock has been explored for well over 100 years. Britain has some of the most varied rock types in the world. These range from fantastic sea cliffs, high mountains and small craggy outcrops next to the roadside. Some of the more famous sites include Stanage Edge in Derbyshire, a gritstone outcrop with some short, world-class routes; the Llanberis Pass in North Wales, with probably the most famous climb of them all, called Cenotaph Corner; Chair Ladder, a golden granite Cornish sea cliff; and Glen Coe in the western Highlands of Scotland.

A climber scales a cliff on the sunny Spanish island of Majorca in the Mediterranean Sea.

These climbers are on a vast rock face in Switzerland. The Swiss Alps have lots of high-altitude climbing.

Europe

European climbers are lucky enough to have a lot of rock to choose from. The Alps are known for their high-altitude climbing. There are also lots of cliff faces in the valleys to climb on. France is probably the single most important climbing country in Europe, both for the enthusiasm of its climbers and for the sheer quality and quantity of its rock. You can climb in Brittany in the north-west, all around the Mont Blanc Alpine region, on the extensive limestone of the Vercors and the Gorge du Verdon in the south, or right down to the Mediterranean coast.

The USA

The USA has some of the best sites in the world, including El Capitan in Yosemite National Park in California, Smith Rocks in Oregon, Joshua Tree out in the high desert, and 'the Gunks' in New York state. The country is huge and these are just a few examples of the climbing that is on offer there.

Australia

Although it is the flattest continent on Earth, Australia makes up for that by having a world-class climbing site. The Arapiles Tooan State Park is known as the best climbing venue in the world. It is in the state of Victoria in the south-east corner of the country. It has a hot summer and warm winter, which means that climbing can take place all year round. The crag is several kilometres long and contains top-quality routes of all grades.

The sun-baked paradise of Arapiles in Australia has over 2,000 climbing routes.

These climbers are high up the vast granite cliffs of Yosemite in California, USA. Yosemite is home to El Capitan, one of the best-known big walls in the world.

29

Glossary

Aerobic exercise Exercise that makes you to breathe heavily and raises your heart rate is aerobic. It refers to the increase in oxygen that your body needs once you start to work hard.

Anchor The point at which a climber attaches to the rock face to make what is called a belay (see below).

Belay The place where a lead climber stops, attaches himself to an anchor to make himself safe, and then brings up his partner on the rope. A belay is also known as a stance.

Belaying This is what you do when you look after your partner while he or she is climbing. You hold the loose end of the rope, which has been attached to a belay device. The device provides the friction for holding a fall.

Bottom roping A climbing system in which the rope goes from the ground up to a sound anchor and back to the ground. The belayer stands on the ground and the climber then ascends the wall and is lowered back down by the belayer.

Bridging This technique involves the climber putting his feet on opposite sides of a wall or rock and standing in balance.

Camming devices Metal pieces of protection that expand and grip the rock when placed into a crack.

Carbohydrates Energy foods, such as potatoes, bread, pasta, rice, sweets and cakes. Wholegrain bread, pasta and potatoes release the energy slowly and so are better for you than sugary foods, which give you a quick fix of energy.

Crag An outcrop of rock in a landscape. Crags often provide excellent climbing.

Dehydrated A person who has lost too much water through heavy exercise and sweating, and has not replaced it by drinking, is dehydrated.

Endurance To be able to do something for a long time.

Grade Some climbs are harder or easier than others. Climbers indicate this by giving each climb a grade.

Granite A hard volcanic rock found on cliffs and mountains all around the world.

Gritstone Gritstone is made from tiny particles of weathered rock laid down millions of years ago. Gritstone provides excellent friction for climbing and is highly prized by climbers.

Hamstring The large tendon that runs from the back of the knee down to the foot. People who exercise a lot but do not stretch afterwards run the risk of getting tight hamstrings.

Lead climbing Climbing a route or pitch, while placing protection as you go. This is more risky than climbing as a second or bottom roping. There is the possibility of a long fall if you come off.

Limestone A rock made from the hard outer shell of tiny sea creatures laid down sea beds millions of years ago.

Multipitch A term that refers to climbs that are longer than a climbing rope. To reach the top, climbers have to make belays on the way up, taking several 'pitches' or rope lengths, to complete the route.

Protein Also know as amino acids, these components of the food we eat make up the muscles and tissue of our bodies. Protein is found in meat, cheese, fish and beans.

Routes A word that climbers use to describe a particular climb. At an indoor climbing wall, routes are often marked out in different colours.

Seconding Once the leader has climbed a route or a pitch on a multipitch route, their partner climbers up after them. They are referred to as the 'second'.

Shake-out Taking a hand or foot off the wall and giving it a good shake to get blood and energy back into it while still on a route, is called having a shake-out.

Sheath The tough outer part of a climbing rope. It protects the more delicate inner white threads of nylon that provide most of the strength and stretch for this vital piece of equipment.

Slab A face of rock that is at an angle that makes it easy to climb. Vertical or over-hanging rock faces are much more difficult to climb.

Top roping Traditionally, this meant belaying a climber from above. However, at most indoor climbing walls this term is also used when belaying from below in the bottom-roping system.

Traversing Movement across a wall or rock face rather than up or down.

Further information

Books to read

Climbing Wall Directory British Mountaineering Council (2008) (This book is published and updated each year)

Extreme Sports: Rock Climbing Chris Oxlade, Lerner Publishing Group (2003)

Radical Sports: Rock Climbing Neil Champion, Heinemann Library (1999)

Rockclimbing: Essential Skills and Techniques Libby Peter, Mountain Leader Training UK (2004)

The Handbook of Climbing Allen Fyffe and Iain Peter, Pelham Books (1990)

Xtreme Sports: Rock Climbing Kate Cooper, Tick-Tock Media Limited (2008)

Useful contacts

British Mountaineering Council
www.thebmc.co.uk

Climbing Australia
www.climbing.com.au

Climb New Zealand
www.climb.co.nz

Mountaineering Council of Ireland
www.mountaineering.ie

The Mountaineering Council of Scotland
www.mountaineering-scotland.org.uk

USA Climbing
www.usaclimbing.net

Websites

The virtual sports library has links to many climbing sites and offers a wealth of information:
http://sportsvl.com/outdoor/climbing.htm

This website offers information on climbing around the world:
www.rockclimbing.com/

This website offers lots of information on indoor climbing, from stretches and cooling down exercises to tips on clothing, equipment and healthy eating:
www.indoorclimbing.com/

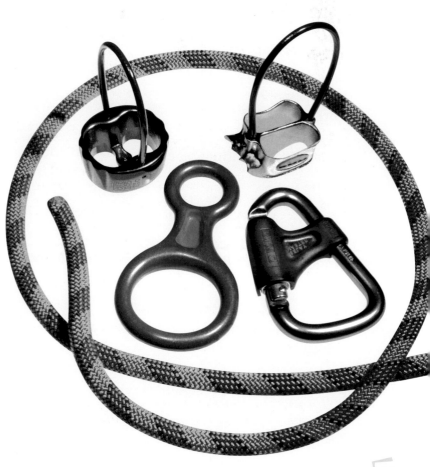

index